Ypsilanti District Library

OUR PLANET

Tundras of the World

Avelyn Davidson

PowerKiDS press

New York

Published in 2009 by The Rosen Publishing Group, Inc.
29 East 21st Street, New York, NY 10010

© 2009 Weldon Owen Education Inc.

All rights reserved. No part of this book may be reproduced in any form without permission in writing from the publisher, except by a reviewer.

Consultant: Colin Sale
U.S. Editor: Erin Heath

Photo Credits: Cover, title page © Shutterstock.com; pp. 4, 14, 20–21 © Bryan and Cherry Alexander; p. 6 Ecocepts International; p. 8 Fred Morris; p. 10 Dan Guravich/O.S.F.; pp. 11, 14–15, 26 Oceania News and Features/Gamma; pp. 12–13 Stefan Lundgren; p. 13 (inset) Frank Todd; pp. 15, 22 Getty Images; p. 17 (top) © John Kelly/Getty Images; p. 17 (bottom) © 2002 Tom Evans/AlaskaStock.com; pp. 18–19 Bryan and Cherry Alexander/Hedgehog House; pp. 24–25 Royal Geographical Society; p. 28 Colin Monteath; p. 29 © P.H.O.N.E./SAOLA.

Illustration Credits: All illustrations © Weldon Owen Inc.

Library of Congress Cataloging-in-Publication Data

Davidson, Avelyn.
　Tundras of the world / Avelyn Davidson.
　　　p. cm. — (Our planet)
　Includes index.
　ISBN 978-1-4358-2817-9 (library binding)
　1. Tundras—Juvenile literature. 2. Tundra ecology--Juvenile literature. I. Title.
　GB571.D38 2009
　551.45'3—dc22
　　　　　　　　　　　　2008034743

Printed in Malaysia

Contents

From Pole to Pole

   The Arctic 4

   Antarctica 6

Animals of the Ice and Snow 8

   Polar Bears 10

   Emperor Penguins 12

Exploring the Arctic 14

Racing on Ice 16

Living in the Ice and Snow 18

The Coldest Town on Earth 20

Exploring Antarctica 22

Against the Odds 24

World Park Antarctica 26

Really Cool Art 28

Glossary 30

Index and Web Sites 32

From Pole to Pole

The two polar regions of the world are unusual and beautiful places, frozen with ice and snow.

The Arctic

The North Pole lies at the northernmost tip of our planet. An ice-covered ocean is surrounded by frozen land called **tundra**, which lies beneath snow for most of the year. This part of the world is called the Arctic.

When temperatures fall as low as -63° F (-53° C), as they can in polar regions, boiling water freezes as soon as it hits the air. It explodes into ice shards.

The Arctic is bordered by an imaginary line called the Arctic Circle. Countries of the Arctic Circle are sometimes called lands of the midnight sun. In midsummer, it is light outside for almost 24 hours of the day. The sun shines even at midnight. In midwinter, it is dark for the same amount of time.

Antarctica

At the opposite end of Earth lies Antarctica. This includes the South Pole. Antarctica is the coldest and iciest place on our planet. Ice, several miles (km) deep in parts, covers all but a few rocky, windswept valleys and the tops of the highest mountains.

Huge **glaciers** spill down the mountains and flow into the oceans surrounding Antarctica. These are frozen solid for much of the year. Sometimes enormous chunks of ice split off and become floating icebergs.

From Pole to Pole continued

WORD BUILDER

The prefixes *ant* and *anti* mean "opposite." Long before Antarctica was discovered, the ancient Greeks thought that there must be a great southern land opposite the land in the north. They were right. Antarctica, or the Antarctic, is at the opposite end of Earth as the Arctic.

Animals of the Ice and Snow

Many animals can live in very cold climates. Some animals spend all year in the ice and snow. Many Arctic animals grow thick, white coats that blend in well with the snow, making the animals hard to see. This helps them hide from animals that eat them. Some animals huddle together or curl up against the bitter cold.

Others hibernate, or sleep, through the winter, living off their stored fat and saving energy by staying still. Others, such as the caribou, **migrate** to warmer places as winter sets in.

Musk oxen have the longest hair of any mammal. Their thick, shaggy coats keep them warm in the icy Arctic weather.

Polar Bears

Polar bears are the giants of the bear family and the largest predators on land. They are well suited to life in the freezing Arctic. A layer of fat keeps them warm in the icy water where they hunt seals. Polar bears are excellent swimmers.

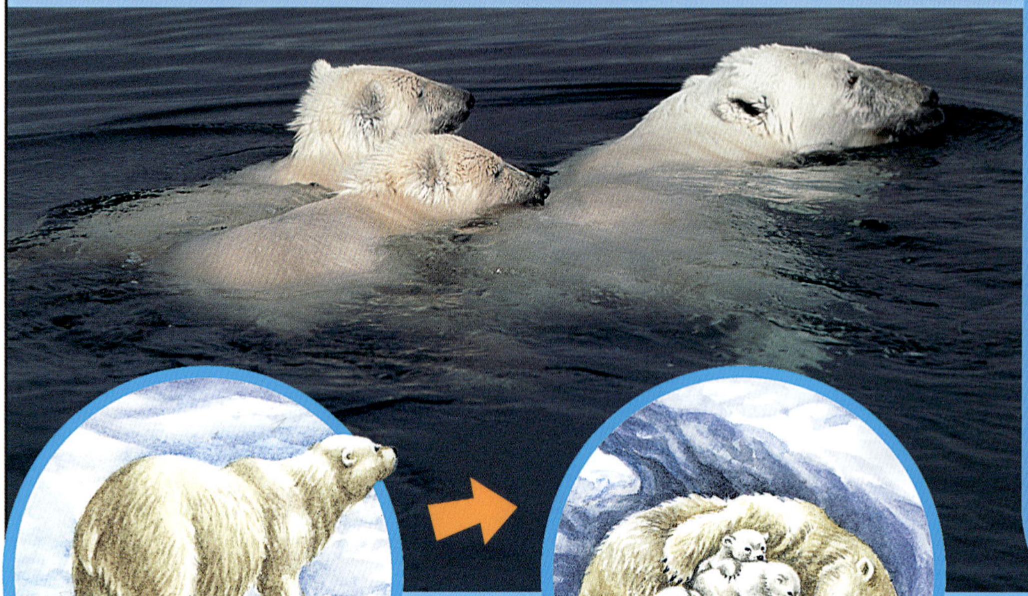

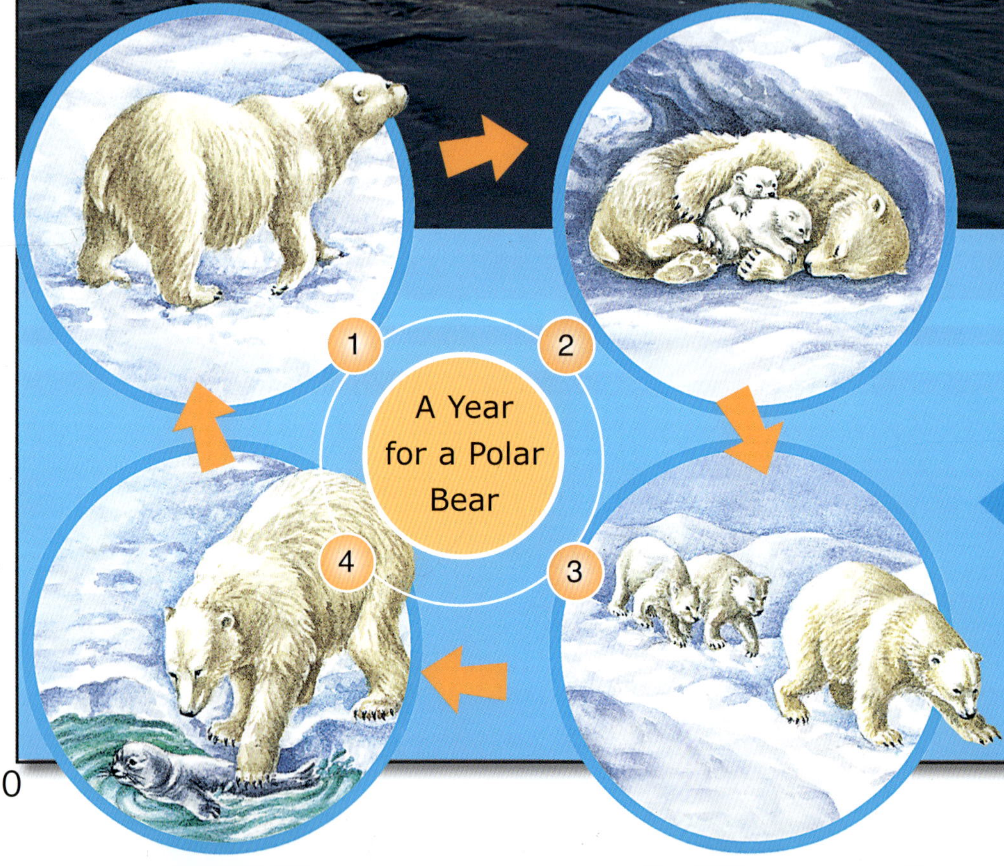

A Year for a Polar Bear

1
2
3
4

Animals of the Ice and Snow continued

Where polar bears live

1. Polar bears usually live on the ice that covers much of the Arctic. Their white fur and skin takes in sunlight for warmth.

2. In late autumn, a female polar bear builds a snow den where she sleeps away the winter months. In midwinter, she gives birth to cubs.

3. In spring, the mother bear brings her cubs out into the open. The cubs stay with their mother for two years.

4. The mother bear protects her cubs and teaches them how to hunt seals.

Emperor Penguins

Emperor penguins live in Antarctica. They are great swimmers. On land, they stay warm in the icy **polar desert** by huddling together in colonies.

Emperor penguin chicks hatch during the cold, bleak Antarctic winter. The mother penguin lays an egg, which the father penguin looks after. He holds the egg on his feet and keeps it warm under folds of fat. The mother penguin then begins a long march to the ocean to feed. She returns two months later when the chick hatches. The father penguin eats nothing this whole time.

| Emperor | Chinstrap | Yellow-eyed | Magellanic |

Animals of the Ice and Snow continued

The mother and father penguin both look after the chick and bring it food. Groups of chicks huddle together while their parents are at sea hunting for fish.

Fjordland   Little (Fairy)

There are 17 kinds of penguins. Emperor penguins are the largest of all and can grow as tall as a seven-year-old child.

13

Exploring the Arctic

Inuit people have made the Arctic areas of Alaska, Canada, and Greenland their home for thousands of years. They are very good at living in the freezing conditions. Long ago, Inuit people lived by hunting fish, seals, whales, and deer. They trained teams of huskies to pull sleds as they moved from place to place.

It wasn't until the 1900s that the first European explorers reached the Arctic and discovered the North Pole. They learned how to stay alive in the ice and snow from the Inuit people.

In the early 1900s, explorers from many countries raced to be the first to reach the North Pole. An American named Robert E. Peary was the first to get there in 1909.

For Peary, it was a case of third time's a charm! His first two attempts failed. Success cost him seven years of hard work and eight of his toes, which he lost to **frostbite**!

Racing on Ice

People are racing for first place in the Arctic ice and snow to this day. Each year, in the frozen wilderness, several winter endurance races take place. Racers choose their own human-powered transportation—skis, mountain bikes, or feet. These races can be as long as 1,100 miles (1,770 km) through subarctic Alaska or Canada in the dead of winter. The racers go over hills, mountain passes, and frozen rivers.

Racing Info

1. Racers must carry or pull all their own gear the whole distance. They must sign in at each checkpoint.

2. Arctic races are very dangerous. People must have first-aid and Arctic survival skills. Temperatures can be as low as -60° F (-51° C). Racers can suffer from frostbite and hypothermia.

3. Racers must be able to light a camp stove and put up a tent in blizzard conditions and in the dark.

4. The same method of transportation must be used for the whole distance.

5. No motors are allowed.

Living in the Ice and Snow

Many people live in the northernmost lands of ice and snow. In Arctic places such as Lapland, there are many modern cities and towns. The people combine old and new ways of life. In Lapland, green, red, and gold lights blaze across the sky during winter. These northern lights are called the aurora borealis, and they are one of nature's most beautiful light shows!

In some places, the Saami people of Lapland still farm herds of reindeer. The deer are important to them for their milk, meat, hides, and bone.

The aurora borealis can be seen in many Arctic Circle countries, but people say the show is best in Lapland!

The colorful national costume that the Saami people often wear honors their family and ancestors.

The Coldest Town on Earth

The coldest town on Earth lies within the Arctic Circle in Siberia, Russia. Here, human breath freezes into ice crystals in an instant, and the frozen ground cracks and bangs like thunder.

Life goes on for the people of the town of Verkhoyansk, even though winter temperatures can drop to -60° F (-51° C). The children simply bundle up in coats, scarves, fur hats, mittens, and reindeer boots to do their chores and go to school!

Lena Potapova thinks Verkhoyansk is the coolest town! She doesn't mind having to break up blocks of ice for her family's water supply.

Lena walks five minutes to school and bundles up to fetch blocks of frozen milk from the local store.

Verkhoyansk

Russia

Exploring Antarctica

There are no native people of Antarctica. Because this great southern land of ice and snow is so far from any other land mass, it was not discovered until the 1800s. It wasn't until later that the first explorers set foot on the continent. When they did, the race for the South Pole was on!

Many great explorers from many different nations set off on long, dangerous **expeditions** to the South Pole. On December 14, 1911, the Norwegian explorer Roald Amundsen and his team became the first people to reach the South Pole.

James Cook | Robert Scott | Ernest Shackleton | Roald Amundsen

Time Line of Early Antarctic Explorers

1772–1775	Captain James Cook **circumnavigates** Antarctica.
Early 1800s	Seal hunters from many different countries explore the oceans and islands around Antarctica.
1901–1904	The first British National Antarctic Expedition is led by explorer Captain Robert Falcon Scott. The men set up a base.
1907–1909	A British expedition led by Ernest Shackleton travels to within 97 miles (156 km) of the South Pole but is forced to turn back because of bad weather.
1910–1911	Norwegian explorer Roald Amundsen and his team become the first to reach the South Pole on December 14, 1911.
1910–1912	Scott's party reaches the South Pole on January 17, 1912, to find the Norwegian flag flying. Scott and his companions die on the return trek.
1914–1916	Sir Ernest Shackleton returns with his team in the *Endurance* on a quest to cross Antarctica from coast to coast. They are caught in **pack ice**.

Against the Odds

"MEN WANTED: for hazardous journey. Small wages, bitter cold, long months of complete darkness, constant danger, safe return doubtful. Honor and recognition in case of success. Sir Ernest Shackleton"

Sir Ernest Shackleton

Would you want a job like this? When the great explorer Sir Ernest Shackleton (shown center) placed the ad above in a London newspaper in 1914, twenty-seven men signed up for the job. They were officers, sailors, surgeons, biologists, geologists, cooks, photographers, and more.

Ernest Henry Shackleton was born in Ireland in 1874. He died in 1922.

With his team, Shackleton set off on an expedition to cross the unmapped continent of Antarctica. The plan went wrong when his ship, the *Endurance*, became stuck on thick pack ice and sank. This left the men stranded in the freezing conditions. Against all odds, Shackleton led his crew to safety. He is remembered as one of the world's greatest leaders.

World Park Antarctica

The journeys of early explorers helped people learn about Antarctica. Today, scientists from all over the world have research stations in Antarctica. They go there to explore and study. Their work can affect the delicate environment, however, so people are thinking of ways to keep Antarctica safe.

In 1959, twelve countries signed a special agreement called the **Antarctic Treaty**. They agreed to protect Antarctica and decided to use it only for peaceful projects. Today, many more countries have signed the treaty, and Antarctica is a park for the world to share.

In Antarctica, temperatures can drop to as low as -128° F (-90° C). Visitors to Antarctica must be careful to leave no waste behind because nothing decomposes in the icy conditions.

27

Really Cool Art

Nature carves beautiful sculptures in the ice and snow of Antarctica. Wind and water are always at work, making new shapes each day.

A world away, in the cold lands of the North, people work hard to make sculptures of their own. During winter carnivals, great blocks of ice are cut and shaped into grand palaces, and artists carve chunks of ice into life-sized figures and scenes.

This ice palace in northern China glows from the inside out! It is lit by neon tubes of purple, pink, blue, and green.

Glossary

Antarctic Treaty (ant-ARK-tik TREE-tee) An agreement that allows people to use Antarctica for peaceful projects only. Members of the Antarctic Treaty protect the plants, animals, and resources of Antarctica. Scientists agree to share their work.

circumnavigate (sur-kum-NA-vuh-gayt) To sail or travel all the way around.

expedition (ek-spuh-DIH-shun) A long journey with a special purpose. During the early 1900s, many brave explorers crossed Antarctica on great expeditions.

frostbite (FROST-byt) When parts of the body freeze. Explorers of the ice and snow must protect

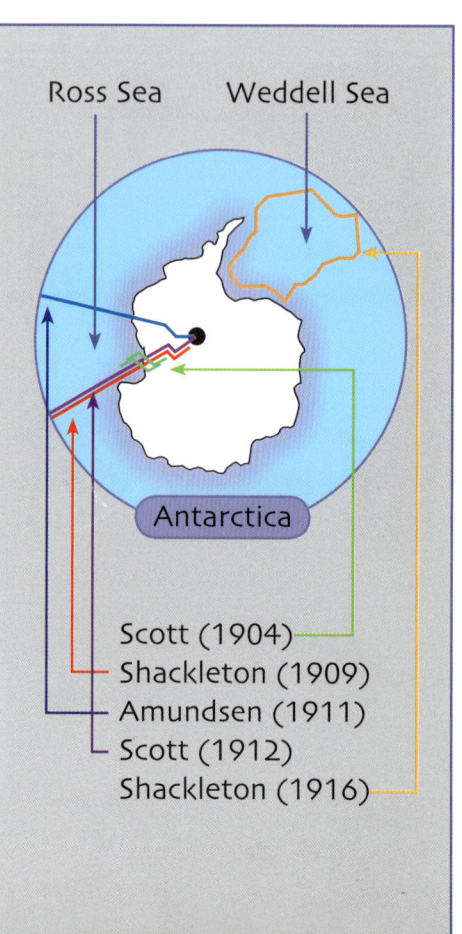

Ross Sea | Weddell Sea
Antarctica
Scott (1904)
Shackleton (1909)
Amundsen (1911)
Scott (1912)
Shackleton (1916)

themselves from frostbite because it can badly damage body parts, such as fingers and toes.

glacier (GLAY-shur) A huge piece of slow-moving ice. Glaciers are found in the poles and in the U-shaped valleys between mountains.

migrate (MY-grayt) To move from one place to another.

pack ice (PAK YS) Huge chunks of sea ice that have been crushed together to form a floating mass of ice.

polar desert (POH-lur DEH-zert) Dry, frozen land where hardly any snow falls.

tundra (TUN-druh) Flat, treeless land where the ground is frozen almost all year long.

Index

Amundsen, Roald	22–23
Antarctica	6–7, 9, 12, 22–28
Antarctic Treaty	26
Arctic	4–5, 8–11, 14–16, 18, 20–21
aurora borealis	18
Cook, Captain James	23
huskies	14
Inuit people	14
Lapland	18–19
North Pole	4–5
Peary, Robert E.	15
penguins	9, 12–13
polar bears	9–11
reindeer	18–19
Saami	18–19
Scott, Captain Robert Falcon	23
Shackleton, Sir Ernest	23–25
South Pole	6–7, 22–23

Web Sites

Due to the changing nature of Internet links, PowerKids Press has developed an online list of Web sites related to the subject of this book. This site is updated regularly. Please use this link to access the list:

www.powerkidslinks.com/opla/tundra/